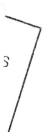

S

# WHAT AM I DOING HERE?

# WHAT AM I DOING HERE?

## Liz Cowley

For my daughter, Katy

*Main illustrations by Dorrance*

*Mood illustrations by Tony Hannaford*
*Design by Prue Fox*

Bene Factum Publishing
PO Box 58122
10 Elm Quay Court
Nine Elms Lane
London
SW8 5WZ

This edition published by Bene Factum

ISBN: 978-1-903071-27-4

# Contents

## I

## At times, I want to scream

## II

## The path of love

# III

## The joys of motherhood

# IV

## They won't ever change

# V

## A woman's lot

# VI

## Senior moments

# I

# AT TIMES, I WANT TO SCREAM

'The more we do, the less they do
in matters of the heart'

# THE CURSE OF CAPABILITY

The trouble, if you're 'capable'-
You don't get fancy things.
You're given a new casserole
But never diamond rings.

The more you do, the less men do
In matters of the heart,
That soft embrace or single rose -
They soon forget the art.

'You're good at that!' they say to you.
You are - so carry on -
Until the day it dawns on you
Their tenderness has gone.

The trouble, if you're 'capable' -
You watch while other wives
Who cannot do a bloody thing
Lead more romantic lives.

'My husband has just bought me this!'
They twirl, in some new dress,
Or showing me a Prada bag.
It irks, I must confess.

And if you also earn your keep,
Well, then it's even worse.
You'll dine out yes, but only Dutch,
He'll empty half your purse.

The more we do, the less they do
In matters of the heart -
The answer is to do much less,
And do that from the start.

# EACH OF US IS AN ISLAND

'All women love …'

I am not all women,
I am me.
And I don't love it.

'What women want…'

Some women.
Not me,
Or anyone else I know.

'Women used to be much happier when…'

Were they?
I wasn't,
And none of my girlfriends were.

'Women always say...'

Do they?
When?
I don't.

'I don't understand women.'

I agree with you there.

# 'DO YOU NOTICE ANYTHING DIFFERENT?'

'You've changed things round.'
'I haven't. Where?'
'Well, was the sofa over there?'

'You've changed your perfume. Mmm, smells good.'
'I've never changed it, never would.'

'Your hair looks different.'
'Does it, how? It's been like this for ages now.'

'Well, nothing round here springs to mind.'
'For goodness sake, you must be blind!'

'You've had a facelift!'
'Thanks a lot. I rather like the face I've got.'

'I'm sorry, nothing I can see.
It all looks much the same to me.'

'For God's sake, darling, try again.
You never notice things, you men.
Or on the rare times that you do,
It's only things that interest *you*.'

# DON'T TELL ME

Tell me about your triumphs,
But add in a fool's endeavour,

Tell me about your baby,
But not how advanced or clever.

Tell me about your virtues,
But add in a couple of vices.

Tell me you're moving houses,
But spare me the moan about prices.

Tell me about your problems,
But not if it takes all day.

Tell me about your travels,
But please put the photos away.

Tell me about your husband,
And tell me about your wife,

But not when you've both come to dinner,
That you long for the single life.

Tell me about your sex life,
But please choose the time and place,

Not when I'm doing the driving,
Or finding a parking space.

And tell me about your parents,
Whether or not they're alive,

But not how they ruined your chances,
When you're way over thirty-five.

## ROUND ROBINS

To all our many precious friends
Who, sadly, live so far away -
May God bless you this Christmas time.
Our greetings from the USA.

This email brings you all the news
And major highlights of the year -
Of course, an invitation too
To take vacations over here.

Exciting news all round the house -
Our floors are now in wood throughout,
So now, when you come out to stay
I won't be scrubbing footprints out.

The church appeal is now complete,
The new roof quite transforms the place,
I have to say, I couldn't pray
With raindrops falling on my face.

My pumpkin patch is doing well -
I grew a dozen giants this fall,
And scored them out at Halloween
They looked quite splendid in the hall.

I still go to the Women's Club -
This year we staged a toddlers' show,
And once again, my brownies won -
1st Prize - the third year in a row.

Bettina's had another child -
Two girls and now a baby boy.
How fortunate her husband Bob
Is Head of Sales at Supertoy.

June wasn't a great month for me -
I had a small lumpectomy,
But thank the Lord I didn't need
To have a full mastectomy.

We made it to the Everglades
As soon as I was feeling well,
And Guy played just like Tiger Woods
Though gators on the greens were hell.

Of course, he's now Vice President
With all Wisconsin on his plate.
We're all so very proud of him -
He's recognized throughout the state.

So, all in all, a busy year
With children, all the usual chores -
I hope that God has been as kind
To those you love, and you and yours.

For further news, please look us up -
We launched our website yesterday.
Click guyandlindyjane.com -
A little treat for Christmas Day!

# DAMN YOU

I've cleared up the table,
I've filled the machine,
I've given the kitchen
A top-to-toe clean.

I've mopped up the floor,
I've put back the chairs,
I've cleaned out the fridge
And brushed up the stairs.

I've done all the laundry,
I've hung it to dry,
I've checked round the house
For things I must buy.

I've planned a month's shopping,
I've made a huge list,
I've checked it three times
For anything missed.

I've driven to Asda,
I've brought a load back,
I've filled up the fridge,
I've made a quick snack.

I've tidied the garage,
I've filled up the car,
I've searched for your spanners,
I've found where they are.

I've rung up the builders,
I've checked out their rates,
I've gone through the diary
And given them dates.

I've fixed up the car
For its next MOT,
I've made a huge cake
For the tennis club tea.

I've brought in the laundry,
The pile is sky high,
I've made us some dinner,
I've done a fish pie.

I've looked up that programme
On BBC3,
I've laid out the table,
And tuned the TV.

I've mown round the garden,
I've watered the flowers,
I've not stopped a moment
For nine or ten hours.

At seven, you're back
And merrily say
'It must be so nice
Doing nothing all day.'

# LATER

'I'll do it later.'
'No, you won't.'
'I will, but later, not just now.'
'You always say you will, then don't,'
'I do! Or else I show you how.'

'I'm free tomorrow, ask me then.'
'And may I know exactly when?
I guess it's up to me again,
It's useless ever asking men.'

'Then don't.'
'I won't.'
'That's good to hear.'
'We'd only have another row.'
'But still, you will.'
'I won't, no point.'
'That settles it!

Both happy now?'

# AT TIMES, I WANT TO SCREAM

I've just rung up the plumber,
He's running two hours late,
He says to ring him later,
Or else to call his mate.

I do - he doesn't answer -
His mobile's not switched on.
I call another plumber -
The company has gone.

And where's the electrician?
I've waited for an hour,
And cannot use the oven,
I'm cut off, with no power.

I need to go out shopping,
But haven't got the car.
They didn't get the parts in,
And walking is too far.

I could get food delivered,
I phone, get stuck on hold -
The kitchen's getting darker,
And worse, it's freezing cold.

So now my dinner party
Has gone right up the spout.
No oven, light or water -
I'll have to take them out.

The nearest decent restaurant
Is four, five miles away.
What's more, it costs a fortune,
And I will have to pay.

And, damn it, I can't drive them,
I'm stuck here with no wheels.
I'll have to get a taxi
Plus fork out for their meals.

I call to book a table.
The answerphone comes on -
Of course, they're shut on Wednesdays,
And all the staff have gone.

At times I feel like screaming
And tearing out my hair -
As soon as you need someone,
They're never ever there.

## QUEUE

His sons take first and second place,
His ex-wife's next at number three,
And I'm behind at four or more -
Today, there's hardly room for me.

You may be in a queue as well -
It's all too common with divorce,
And find the whole thing equal hell;
You find out far too late, of course.

His grown-up sons live out in Spain.
I say 'I'd love to go to France'.
But every year it's Spain, again -
My choice of where to go? No chance.

And there, I slip to number seven.
I babysit for three small boys.
He finds his little grandsons heaven,
And loads them with expensive toys.

He takes his offspring out to bars.
I tidy up behind their wives,
And can't help getting very cross,
Comparing all our numbered lives.

He gives them money, buys them cars,
But ever buy a car for me?
What makes me even madder still -
He's just bought one for number three.

I live with him, he lives with guilt,
I'm trapped by all that went before.
I'll always be at four or more -
Whatever did I marry for?

# DRAMA QUEENS

Although I love Hattie,
She drives me quite batty.
She never has time to hear what I say.
Each time I meet her,
As soon as I greet her
She talks of a string of disasters all day.

It's all so dramatic -
The mice in the attic,
The horrors of Heidi, her latest au pair,
The cost of the plumber,
The weather this summer,
The problems she's had with her teeth and her hair.

The painter, the builder,
The bills that half-killed her,
The fact they did nothing each time she was out.
I wish she'd be calmer,
But Hattie loves drama,
I can't get a word in with Hattie about.

The children, the school fees,
The state of her oak trees,
The cost of repairing her Chippendale chair,
Her husband, his heart pills,
The cat's ills, the vet's bills,
The neighbour whose visits are driving her spare.

Her nieces, her nephews,
Her problems with refuse -
'If only the council would come once a week.'
The garbage, the mortgage,
The state of her marriage,
The taps in the bathroom that sprung a huge leak.

I listen astonished,
And if I admonished
Her one-way orations, and why they aren't fair,
She'd say I was selfish,
Clam up like a shellfish,
And sit there all sulky, or say I don't care.

I wish she'd be calmer,
But Hattie loves drama,
She lives her whole life as if in a play.
She loves a disaster -
Though all mine go past her -
She never has time to hear what I say.

I hate to sound catty,
But each time with Hattie,
I welcome the moment she's up and away.
She never once guesses
That all she confesses
Will leave me a wreck for the rest of the day.

## SELF-HELP SEMINARS

I hate the sort of seminar
That finds out 'who we truly are'
And points us to 'our true vocation'.
I'm sure there are much better ways
To find ourselves than days and days
Of endless 'inner exploration'.

There's nothing wrong with having goals,
But sitting round with worthy souls
For days of heavy introspection?
I'd rather simply sit at home
And let imagination roam
Indulging in some calm reflection.

'Your chance to find out who you are!' -
I can't, well, not without a bar.
Can you sip Perrier all day,
And go without a cigarette?
By lunchtime I begin to fret
And work out how to slip away.

At seminars, I get depressed -
I'm always at my worst, not best.
They somehow make my spirits sink,
And make me want a good, stiff drink.
The less I search within myself,
The happier I am, I think.

## CHARITY DINNERS

The man on my left is a banker,
The chap on my right is in law.
We've been at our table five minutes,
Already the evening's a bore.

I can't hear the rest of my neighbours.
The problem? The ceiling's too low -
I think it's called 'presbyacusis'
When ambient sounds tend to go.

The others seem suitably chatty,
Apparently having some fun,
Or perhaps they're just making an effort?
I'd ask them, but that isn't done.

The programme says 'Sounds of the Sixties'
And jiving to 'Joe's Funky Band',
And before that, a Charity Auction
To raise around twenty-five grand.

The bidding will start in the hundreds,
And that counts me out, for a start.
I know it's a wonderful gesture,
But dull if you can't play a part.

I look at the menu with horror -
Four or five courses at least.
My waist-band is bursting already,
The last thing I want is a feast.

I long to be making an omelette,
And watching a soap on TV.
The whole thing will drag on for ages -
At least til a quarter past three.

I glue on a smile until pudding,
And that's at a quarter past ten.
The banker is driving me crazy -
He's telling the same joke again.

The loo? What a wonderful answer!
I'll escape by the speech at eleven.
The taxi will take forty minutes
And the ride will be absolute heaven.

# COMPARISONS

'Oh, what a darling little house.
You've found yourself a little gem!'
She means that theirs is twice the size
And I am not as rich as them.

'This sitting room is oh, so sweet,
And all your old things fitted in.'
She means, why keep that threadbare junk?
It's high time for the wheelie bin.

'Well, who wants all that space like us?
Our drawing room drives me to tears.'
She means that's only when she's charged
For cleaning twenty chandeliers.

'Two bedrooms? Perfect! All you need.
Who wants a crowd to come and stay?'
She means their house fits dozens in,
And half the world on Christmas Day.

'You've even brought your old TV.
Who needs a flat screen anyway?'
She means that she has two or three,
And chucked the ones like mine away.

'Oh look, a little patio -
It's perfect for a barbecue!'
She means that their estate is huge,
And also has a splendid view.

'Downsizing…such a clever move.
I so admire your bravery.'
She means she'd hate to do the same
And couldn't stand to live like me.

# IF ONLY I DARED TELL HER

You have to move on,
Realise when things have gone.
Can't stay in your past for ever,
Have to live for now, or never.
You have to move on.

Stop talking of ten years ago
And someone I will never know.
All that talking makes you sapped
And keeps all those ambitions trapped.
You have to move on.

It's never more than half a day
Before you turn to me and say
'It's so unfair what he has done',
You always feel that he has 'won'.
It's over, finished, dead and gone -
You have to move on.

Can't you see these conversations
Are stopping future inspirations?
Can't you see it's draining, wearing
All these endless hours comparing
How he's doing, how you're faring?
You have to move on.

Divorce, my love, is nothing new,
We've all been through the same as you,
But chose to do what you can't do.
Forget the past and start anew.
You have to move on.

## 'HAVE YOU HEARD THE ONE ABOUT …?'

I cannot stand the sort of bloke
Who longs to tell the latest joke,
Especially when we're on our own,
Or, worse still, on the telephone.

'I heard this cracker at the pub.'
'And here's one from the rugby club!'
Please, more than one joke hurts my head,
And bad ones strike libido dead.

Jokes always take the time away
From better things to hear or say,
And slice a chap's appeal in half
While watching out for when to laugh.

And jokes I don't get at the end
Can truly drive me round the bend.
It's even worse when they explain
Or take you through the joke again.

I do my best, applaud each joke,
But rapidly go off a bloke
Who waits to hear a peal of laughter,
Then tells another joke straight after.

## 'IF I WERE YOU'

I'm quite amazed what people say
When asked to France to come and stay.
It must be travel that's to blame -
At home they'd never say the same.

'If I were you', 'If I were you',
'If I were you', 'If I were you' -
It only takes a day or two
Before they tell me what to do.

'If I were you, I'd dump that shower -
It's useless, never any power.
One other thing, if I were you,
I'd add another bathroom, too'.

'This sink is awful, such a pain -
You must have noticed, doesn't drain.'
'It's ancient!' 'Yes, the plumbing too -
I'd chuck it out, if I were you'.

'I'd change this to a breakfast bar -
A folding one - pulled out this far.
If I were you, I'd want more space,
This counter clutters up the place'.

'Your patio needs sorting out,
Too many bloody trees about.
A chop is surely overdue -
I'd want more view if I were you'.

'You see that pot - there - on the lawn?
Well, on its own it looks forlorn.
I'd make a group if I were you -
And add another one or two'.

'And don't your floors need sorting out?
You only need a pot of grout
To make them look as good as new.
I'd start today, if I were you'.

'That Persian rug is lovely, dear -
But frankly, it looks wrong out here.
I have to say, if I were you,
I'd hide it in the downstairs loo'.

'And on the subject of the loo,
The French might think it's rude of you
To have a sketch of Waterloo -
I'd take it down if I were you'.

Of course I know what I should do -
Reply 'Well, thanks. But I'm not you,
And if I were, I'd never say
'If I were you' ten times a day'.

## MOANING MINNIE

She doesn't get on with her mother,
And now they don't speak any more.
She's always at odds with her brother,
And ditto her sister-in-law.

She can't stand her daughter's new husband,
So now she's estranged from the two,
And complains that they don't want to see her,
Although their first baby is due.

She's quarrelled for years with her sister,
All contact stopped ages ago,
And whinges about her ex-husband,
And everyone else that I know.

She feels the whole world is against her.
Of course, she's the one in the right,
And if I invite her to dinner
She goes on complaining all night.

She won't see the family at Christmas,
And no-one will visit or phone,
And that means that I'll have to ask her,
Or else she'll be left all alone.

There's always a crisis or problem,
But one that she simply can't see.
If only she'd ever admit it,
And say that 'The problem is me'.

## BABY TALK

For months and months we didn't meet,
And then I saw her in the street -
'Hello Jemima, how are you?
And goodness me, your baby too!'
(I'd quite forgotten she was due.)

'You tell her, Jubbly Bubbliboo!
Give Liz a little word or two.
She's so advanced, my Bubbliboo.
Already she can talk to you!'

'Um, how about a spot of lunch?
I know a pub that does a brunch.
It's only fifty yards away,
And full of buggies every day.'

'I'll ask her - Jubbly Bubliboo,
Well, can we spare an hour or two?
You tell your Mumsy what to do.
Oh no, she says her feed is due!

You're starving, aren't you Bubliboo?
You can't hang on til half past two!
You always know what's best for you,
You clever girl, you always do!'

'Oh dear. I guess I'll say goodbye.'
'Well, say goodbye then, Bubliboo.
Oh look, a smile, that's nice of you,
And wow, a little wave or two!'

I say goodbye, go on my way,
With some relief, I have to say.
I never did like newborns much
With mothers who speak double Dutch.

# DROWNING

I am going under in a sea of sympathy
And watery voices.
The English cannot speak the language of death.
Friends cannot even speak your name.

Some cannot speak at all.
Sometimes, they sail by on the other side of the street,
Silently hoping I haven't seen them,
Supportive, but stuck for what to say.

Sanity is the supermarket,
And the solace of strangers who never knew you.
Managing throws me a lifebelt.
Saucepans need to be washed up,
The house is a never-ending tide of laundry,
And mess keeps my head above water.

A flood of invitations arrives on the doormat.
I am asked to dinners where everybody keeps death
And holidays off the menu.
They think I must keep in the swim.

Maybe I should get away,
Perhaps back to where it happened.
I could even send jolly postcards
To prove I'm a survivor.
'Writing this on the beach,
Just had a dip, the water's lovely!'

Ever since your death I have been drowning
In a wave of kindness.

# SOMETIMES, YOU JUST HAVE TO SHUT UP

She may be bright, she may be smart,
I'm sure some  others find her fun.
But not me. Why? She floats downstairs
When all the washing up is done.
She's thirtyish, been married twice,
She's now fed up with number two.
Of course, she's cleaned him out of cash -
The one thing she knows how to do.

He doesn't know she's leaving him,
Though all her girlfriends seem to know,
Which makes it hard to talk to him -
Well, places that you dare not go.
Two kids, the first one traumatized,
Impossible, and missing Dad.
And turned down by a load of schools;
I'm not surprised, the times he's had.

The second child? Well, fine right now.
But sure to end up like her brother,
And play up when her father's gone,
And far prefer him to her mother.
And then what, husband number three?
I guess so, as she'll want the cash.
And when that's gone, she'll soon move on,
And find herself another stash.

She's always in designer gear,
From top to toe immaculate,
And never helps to do a thing,
While others all get on with it.
Why bother then? Why have her round?
Why put up with the agony?
Quite simple. She's my daughter's friend.
'Please Mum, be nice to her, for me'.

# II

# THE PATH OF LOVE

'You're not for me;
that's all too plain to see'

# AGONY AUNT

My problem is this boy at school.
We went out a whole term, you see,
But now I'm feeling such a fool,
Because he never talks to me.

I lie awake and cry all night
And try and work out what to do,
But nothing ever works out right,
So now I need advice from you.

Please, could you put me on your page,
And soon, before it's all too late?
And if you need to know my age,
Well, I am seven, he is eight.

## STRANDED

You washed over me
Like the sea over a pebble,
Smoothing the jagged edges
And bringing out the secret colours
I never knew I had.

Suddenly stranded, I have dried dull.
Grey, un-noticed, leached, beached.
No-one picks me up
Because no light is reflected back,
And I am far away from the tide.

Friends tell me to get back into the sea of things.
But I need a strong hand to throw me back there,
And I fear I will be dropped again.

# WHAT A BUMMER

He's friendly,
He's kind,
He's warm
And he's witty.
He earns enough money,
He works in the City.

He's clever,
He's charming,
The right age for me.
I'd say around thirty -
At most, thirty-three.

He's sporty,
He's hunky,
The same gym as me,
He's interested too -
That's easy to see.

He's focused, attentive,
And all eyes for me.
He's single as well -
He told me he's free.

On top of all that,
He's tall and he's slim.

God, what a bummer, I don't fancy him.

## ODE TO A BLIND DATE IN A CLUB

My heart sinks, and a heavy dullness pains
My head, as though already I were drunk
Or emptied all last dreams into the drains
One minute past, and ever downwards sunk.
You're not for me; that's all too plain to see;
Quite vanished, any hopes I had before,
But say hello I must, and talk to you,
Despite my urge to grab my bag and flee
Unshackled, single, flying through the door
And faster than a blind date ever flew.

You've seen my Facebook photo, there's the rub;
I said that I'd be here at five to ten.
I told you I'd be waiting in the club,
And now I've made the same mistake, again.
You've spotted me, and now I'm stuck. You smile.
I groan inside, just as I've done before.
My chance to flee is over, now too late,
Despite my instant urge to run a mile.
I know at once you'll be a crashing bore.
Whyever did I say I'd be your date?

You're not my type; I see at once that's true,
The way you look and dress, and ogle me,
But say hello I must, and talk to you,
Wherever else that I might yearn to be.
I ape sweet smiles and carefree happiness,
Whilst forced to spend an hour or even more
Of drinking, chatting to a hopeless case,
And liking you each minute less and less
As on and on you bore and try to score
And make me scream for some far distant place.

*With apologies to John Keats and 'Ode to a Nightingale'*

## UP IN SMOKE

The nicest gift I ever had
Was posted through my door -
A pack of twenty cigarettes
Was lying on the floor.

You'd opened it, penned messages
On each and every one -
'I love you, darling', words like that.
So touching, what you'd done.

What's more, because you never smoked,
And found the risks alarming,
Your gift to me was twice as nice,
I found it doubly charming.

I kept that pack for years and years
Tucked in my bedside table,
And never smoked a single one.
I marvelled I was able.

Each time when out of cigarettes,
Not once did I succumb.
I always kept the pack intact
And pottered out for some.

But when you cheated, that was it,
Revenge was swift and vicious.
I smoked the lot in front of you -
All twenty were delicious.

## ALONE ON VALENTINE'S DAY

Roses, roses everywhere, but not one stem for me,
Champagne, champagne everywhere,
But nowhere that I'll be,
Card shops, card shops everywhere,
And hearts beyond computing,
And cupids, cupids everywhere,
On ads when I'm commuting.

Restaurants, restaurants everywhere,
Each table for a twosome,
Couples, couples everywhere, it's absolutely gruesome,
Lovers, lovers everywhere, but not the man for me,
And love films, love films everywhere,
All night on my TV.

Mothers, mothers everywhere,
Who care for those alone,
And wonder how to ease your day,
And whether they should phone.
You get one card - no signature -
And ask them if they sent it.
They tell you 'No' - they did, you know -
And God, how you resent it.

## ANOTHER WOMAN

You're silent so often, and then won't explain.
I've tried to ask why, but I won't ask again,
I know you won't tell me; it's always in vain.

You turn away often when I look at you,
As if there's a secret; you say that's not true.
You laugh, and you tell me that everything's fine,
That if there's a problem, the problem is mine.

You talk with such ease if I'm not in your space,
But then, when I am, there's a change in your pace,
As if you have wandered to some other place -
Your absence is written all over your face.

You're distant, on edge, abrupt, often rude,
Endless mercurial changes of mood.
I know what's behind it, behind all the change,
I know why it is your behaviour's so strange.

I know you're in love, that's easy to see.
I don't know with whom -
Except it's not me.

## MAKING LOVE

Men think making love is like driving a car -
That anyone can do it, and it all comes naturally.
It doesn't, so neither do we.

If only it were like driving a car.
Then they'd all get proper lessons
And a decent instructor.

And more of them would pass the test.

## IN PRAISE OF ABSENCE

I didn't like you much at first -
I think you knew.

You persevered, you carried on
A year or two.

And then you gave up, went away -
What else to do?

At once I wished that you were back,
And so did you.

You came, we started off again,
This time, anew.

And then, I liked you more and more.
It grew and grew.

And now it's love, and growing still -
We're good, we two.

## THE SNAKE

I saw her just the other day -
As usual, coiled arond her prey.
I didn't ask about her life,
Or his - because I know his wife.

She slithers into new affairs,
And always bites them in the bud.
Then quickly hunts out ready spares -
My ex is on her trail of blood.

She slides and glides along her way
Without a thought for whom she's hurting,
And leaves her victims one by one -
While they are planning, she's deserting.

But then I saw, good God above,
The reptile seemed to be in love!
And he will never leave his wife -
She lets him lead an open life.

I watched the way she clung to him -
It's clear, this time the snake is smitten.
I smile, revenge is more than sweet.
A snake hurts too when it is bitten.

# TICK, TOCK

Tick, tock,
Tick, tock -
I hear it now,
The body clock.

Coming up to thirty-three,
Still can't find the man for me.
Thought I had; it all went wrong.
Wish I hadn't stayed so long.

Gone beyond the twenties stage -
Guess I'm fussy at my age.
If a new guy comes along,
Always finding something wrong.

Met some new chaps, two or three.
Best one didn't fancy me.
Sometimes used to call or text,
Nothing ever happened next.

Tell myself to try again,
Never meet the decent men.
Only ones who come my way
Are in relationships or gay.

Girlfriends married, moved away,
Harder meeting up today.
Some are Mums, same age as me,
Most with children one to three.

Tick, tock,
Tick, tock,
It's getting loud, the body clock.

## I THINK IT'S TIME WE GOT MARRIED

'I think it's time we got married.
How long is it, twenty-five years?
A splendid excuse for a party
Before we turn into old dears.'

'Yes, I think it's time we got married,
There's a risk of us missing the bus.
However, one problem, my darling -
Just who would get married to us?'

## THANK YOU

I thank the other woman
Who stole my chap away.
Without her intervention,
I'd still be there today.

I thank the other woman
Who's now his second wife,
And so does my new husband,
I'll thank you all my life.

## WHY CAN'T WE TALK PROPERLY?

We talk a different way today,
We do not answer straight away.
Instead we wait before we do
At least a day, or maybe two,
Or, if we feel at all unsure,
Three days or four, or even more.
And then, if we get no reply,
We sigh and try to work out why,
And who should break the silence next.
We speak a different language -
Text.


## IF ONLY YOU WOULDN'T

You use all the tissues,
You muck up the basin,
You shave in the water
I'm washing my face in.

You never go shopping,
You lag when we're walking,
You choose when I'm dozing
To feel just like talking.

You panic in airports -
They make you neurotic,
You always buy pants
That are so unerotic.

You use the whole kitchen
When making a snack,
And never once ever
Put anything back.

You scrumple the papers
And hog the best section,
You choose when I'm sleeping
To have an erection.

You go on a diet
And then go on binges,
And I have to listen
To weight-watching whinges.

You wake up at night
With a sound that's quite hellish,
You say it's a dream,
But you never embellish.

You go back to sleep
In no time at all,
And leave me awake
To stare at the wall.

You empty your ashtrays
In places you shouldn't -
Like baskets with holes in.
If only you wouldn't.

If only you wouldn't.
If only you wouldn't.
But leave you, I couldn't -
I love you, I shouldn't.

## GOING NOWHERE

'Where's it all going?' she finally said,
This time reluctant to get into bed.

'Hopefully, nowhere at this time of night.
Now, get into bed, and turn out the light.'

'Don't be facetious.  You know what I mean.
Six years? Or seven? How long has it been?'

'Please get into bed and turn out the light.
You know I can't talk at this time of night.

I hear what you say, but don't ask me now,
You know it will only lead to a row.

Why do you choose to ask me this late?
You know I'm on call at twenty to eight.

Now turn out that light and get into bed.
And do it right now - you heard what I said.

Where's it's all going? Who needs a plan?
Why can't a woman think like a man?'

# NEIGHBOURS

'My place or yours?' he finally said,
Not asking,
Assuming they would share a bed.
It was the way she liked it best -
Assumption made her feel undressed.
But she thought for a second as she watched his face,
Picturing him,
What it meant,
His place…

The bed, too large, with its black silk cover,
Somehow suggesting a practised lover.
The rug,
A deep, enveloping fur.
It was him, not her.

Her place,
Where he had learned to please,
Where he handled her with unnerving ease,
But on her terms.

'Mine', she said.

Tonight she didn't want the pictures of erotic poses
As much as the bedside bowl of roses,
And the pinks and blues he'd never choose,
And the clothes-strewn chairs and the scented airs.

Tonight, she would be mistress of her own place,
Making him keep her pace.

No more words were said as she shut his door
And slipped softly across the corridor.

## TELL ME WHY

Whatever did I say
To make you walk away?

Something that I said
Or did, perhaps in bed?

A side of me you saw
To make you slam the door?

You've met somebody new?
I guess that could be true.

I cannot work out why
You went with no goodbye.

You didn't even text,
I'm totally perplexed.

I wish that you would say
What made you walk away.

It's awful not to know
Why lovers choose to go.

It's always far worse pain
If no-one will explain.

What stopped you loving me?
I hate a mystery.

# AFTER THE OFFICE PARTY

How stupid, what madness, why did I say
'I'll give you a lift, I'm driving your way?'

And why did I stop to have a last drink?
I'm now in his flat, so what must he think?

He's achingly gorgeous, far younger than me -
I think someone mentioned he's just twenty-three.

He's flirting quite clearly, that is for sure.
I tell myself 'Don't - you've turned forty-four'.

I'll say he's a baby, that I need to go -
And what will he tell me? Already I know.

He'll whisper, so charming, my age doesn't scare.
He'll say, so disarming, that he doesn't care.

I'll pause for a second and think of his bed,
And yes, I'll be tempted to go straight ahead.

I don't, and then fleetingly feel somewhat sad,
But know by tomorrow that I will be glad.

I smile to myself as I close his front door.
Tomorrow is safe. I'm his boss, like before.

# WHY DO YOU ANNOY ME?

Why do you annoy me?
Let me count the ways.

I do all the cooking,
Mostly without praise.

I do all the gardening,
You won't even mow.

Where's it kept, the mower?
Well, do you even know?

I do all the shopping,
Otherwise, we'd starve.

And, at Sunday lunches,
It's me who has to carve.

I lay up the table,
And clear the things away.

Raise yourself to help me?
That would be the day.

Why then do I love you?
Goodness only knows.

Must be too forgiving,
Good-natured, I suppose.

## RIGHT PLACE, WRONG MAN

Venice.
A thousand angels stare down from gilt ceilings
On a tide of tourists
Stuffing ten centuries into three days,
While I look around
Miserably.

I am lost in your life support of trippers
And lovers with locked hands,
While mine are in my pockets.

A maid dusts a window,
Vanishes like another of your ghosts.
I wish I could disappear that easily.

A cat squints into the sun.
Shuttered windows stare out like blind eyes,
While mine are hidden behind dark glasses.

People pass,
Bloated with culture and pasta,
And I am heavy with foreboding.

How can I get through another night?

## INSECURITY

Greater than my love for you
Is fear of ever losing you.
I wish I didn't live this way,
In constant dread that you will stray.

It seems that nothing that you say
Can ever drive that fear away.
It seems there's isn't any cure
For always feeling insecure.

What makes me yearn for you to say
You love me, twenty times a day?
Why is it that I can't believe
That you will never want to leave?

Unless I like myself much more,
I'll push you through the exit door.
I know you'll start to find it boring,
All your endless reassuring.

If only I could lose this fear,
If only I could see that day.
My greatest fear is fear itself
Will end up driving you away.

## THE SHOE

Just like a child, I'm learning how
To tie the laces on a shoe
And slowly walk away from you.
I'm learning how to tie the laces
And every day improving now
And managing a few more paces.

I have no teacher at my side,
I have no friendly voice to say
'You're doing pretty well today.'
I have no solid hand to grip,
Or guide to see how hard I've tried,
And grasp me if I start to slip.

The next time that I see your face -
I surely will, some place, some day -
You'll find me walking in a way
That tells you clearly I've come through.
You'll marvel at my strength and pace,
And know that I am over you.

Just like a child, I'm learning how
To tie the laces on a shoe
And slowly walk away from you.
And when at last I learn to run -
I will, I'm walking faster now,
You'll never spot a lace undone.

# ON THE SIDE

You often talk about divorce,
You shouldn't.
I know that you will never split,
You couldn't.
You say you long to leave your wife,
You don't.
You say one day you'll marry me,
You won't.
The children keep you where you are,
They should.
You cannot make that sort of choice,
I could.
If you loved me as I love you,
You would.
You say you're always there for me,
You aren't.
You tell me not to call your home,
I shan't.
But leave you, as I know I should?
I can't.

## MY DOG

I sometimes think I love my dog
A little more than I love you.
He looks at me with melting eyes,
And in a way you never do.

He always longs to share my bed,
But sleeps outside the bedroom door,
And barks with joy when let inside,
While you roll over, grunt and snore.

I sometimes think I love my dog
A darned sight more than you love me.
When did you last come out for walks,
Or snuggle up against my knee?

He stares at me with blinding trust,
And always greets me at the door.
I think there was a time you did,
But never see that any more.

You bark when people come and stay,
He only does to say hello,
And he looks sad while you look glad
When it's the time to see them go.

While he'd defend me to the death,
Would you? I have to say, I doubt it.
And when I scold him, unlike you,
He learns, and doesn't sulk about it.

You wag your finger, he his tail,
And always welcomes all his meals,
And never bores me with his moans,
And how he thinks, or how he feels.

Each time, when I go out to shop,
You always find a get-out wheeze,
While he bounds out, all wriggling glee,
Jumps in the car, and sniffs the breeze.

I'll always love my dog and you,
I'll always love you both for sure -
But when I think about my dog,
I sometimes think I love him more.

## I'M STILL YOUR GREATEST SUPPORTER

'I can't believe you'd say that.'
'I can't believe you'd feel that.'
'I can't believe you'd do that,
That's not what I would do.'

'I can't believe you'd hope that.'
'I can't believe you'd want that.'
'I can't believe you'd think that,
That wouldn't be my view.'

'I can't believe you'd wish that.'
'I can't believe you'd dream that'.
'I can't believe you've done that -
But still believe in you.'

## A HUGE HOLE

I am sitting in the kitchen
With my third glass of wine,
Staring blankly into space.
You have left a huge hole.

Twenty years together,
But you had to go.
Your burned through a fortune,
And left us penniless.

But how can I live without you?
Farewell, my beloved Aga.

## IT'S NEVER TOO LATE

On my first week in Martinique
I met a lady in a hat -
A truly splendid hat at that,
It made my heart go pit-a-pat.

By Jove, I thought, that hat's a winner,
And asked the lady out to dinner.
She wore the hat the whole way through,
A very charming thing to do.

The dinner was a great success.
I fell for her, I must confess.
I loved her smile, I loved the hat,
And I proposed, and that was that.

Oh yes, I know I'm eighty-three.
The good thing is, that so is she.
I thought that you might like to know
We're Juliet and Romeo.

This postcard comes with hugs and kisses
From Grandpa and his future Mrs.

# III

# THE JOYS OF MOTHERHOOD

'Our happiness is intertwined'

## PUSHY MUMS

Please, mothers, could you keep your prams
Beside you when you cross the road?
Not sticking out in front of you -
A certain way to lose the load.

Please, mothers, could you pull, not push,
When crossing roads with traffic near?
Or else the handles may be left,
But not much of your little dear.

# THE COMFORTER

My daughter had a comforter
That started white as snow,
And everywhere my daughter went,
It, too, was sure to go.

The park, the zoo, the infant school,
The comforter was there,
And soon attracted slime and grime
And strands of toddler hair.

The comforter was chewed and sucked
Until it went quite black,
And always stuffed within her mouth -
I couldn't wrench it back.

However hard I tried and tried
To keep it nice and clean,
I could not prise the rag away
Without a ghastly scene.

The rag went stiff, with quite a whiff,
And then it started moulting.
Your daughter may have had one too,
And isn't it revolting?


*With apologies to my daughter, and to Mary and her little lamb*

# TANTRUMS

The best advice I ever had
Came from a Mrs Vinegrad,
Who told me that an angry child
Can easily become more wild
If tantrums lead to conversations
In which to talk through their frustrations.
You make them objects of attention.
That's what the 'experts' never mention.

That happened with my youngest son.
He always had the greatest fun
While telling us, for what seemed ages,
About what lay behind his rages.
And what, precisely, made him mad.
It only made him twice as bad.

These days, experience has shown
It's best to leave him well alone.
The 'experts' tell you, 'talk things through' -
The very worst thing you can do.

So, thank you, Mrs Vinegrad -
The best advice I ever had.

# EMBARRASSING HABITS

So embarrassing was Billy,
Always playing with his willy.
The times his mother had to say,
While people tried to look away,
'Please Billy, not in public, dear.
It's not polite with people here.'

One weekend, at a social do,
She fell upon an answer new,
By handing him two party trays
With fine arrays of canapés.
With both hands busy, thus young Billy
Had none left over for his willy.

This big success was soon repeated,
And, in the end, all but deleted
The vexing habit Billy had
Which always drove his mother mad.
So, no surprise when ten years later,
Young Billy chose to be a waiter.

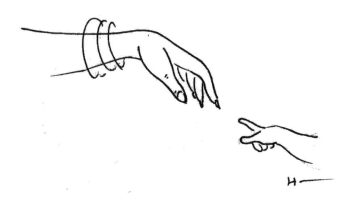

## MOTHERS AND DAUGHTERS

What powerful creatures daughters are,
And how much more their state of mind.
When mine is happy, so am I,
Our happiness is intertwined.
But if the opposite is true
And she is sinking ever down,
I lift a hand to keep her up
But struggle as my spirits drown.
What powerful creatures daughters are,
What powerless mothers we can be.
However do we carry on
While witnessing their misery?

# A TEENAGE DAUGHTER

'Dear Santa, please bring some Chanel,
Oh yes, and Calvin Klein as well,
Or Kenzo might have something new.
You couldn't take a look, could you?

A Joseph jacket would be great,
And, Santa, since I'm always late,
A watch by Tiffany would do.
I'd also love a Swatch or two.

Please, Santa dear, no more CDs,
These days, I'm into DVDs.
Some chocolates would be nice as well -
Rum truffles please, by Charbonnel.

Manolo Blahnik shoes are chic -
I saw some brilliant ones last week.
And, Santa, this year, please try harder
To find a beaded purse from Prada.
That's a perfect stocking-filler.

With love and kisses from Camilla.'

# I WANT TO BE A MODEL

Thirteen years, thirteen years,
Thirteen years onward,
Dreaming of modelling,
Girls by the hundred.

Make-up to right of them,
Hair gels to left of them,
Mirrors in front of them,
Jars by the hundred.

Sadly so innocent, sadly so innocent,
How could they ever know how many blundered?
Theirs not to reason why,
Theirs just to beautify,
Hours by the hundred.

Skin creams to right of them,
Toners to left of them,
Shampoos in front of them,
Mags by the hundred.

Dreams of the model scene,
Years before seventeen,
How could they ever know
Thousands have blundered?

School at the back of them,
Home at the back of them,
Friends at the back of them,
All of it plundered.

*With apologies to Alfred, Lord Tennyson, and
The Charge of the Light Brigade*

## BATHROOM MIRROR

'Bathroom mirror on the wall,
Who is the fairest of us all?'

'You - I tell you every day.
What else am I supposed to say?

You gaze at me the whole damned time.
And may I please complete my rhyme?

You've been in here at least an hour.
Your parents might just like a shower.

Could I perhaps suggest to you
My fellow mirror in the loo?'

## LISTEN TO YOURSELF

'In my day…' 'What I say…' 'I wish you could see…'
'We're worried about you, your father and me.'

'Of course we're both proud that you've got a degree,
 But three years of parties won't make a CV.'

'You could look so handsome, without all that stubble.
 Is shaving old-fashioned, or just too much trouble?'

'We know it's much harder to find a good job.
 But surely it helps if you don't look a slob?'

'And, as your father has so often said,
 It might be a help if you got out of bed.'

'And may I remind you, we're not an hotel?
 I've quite enough washing, without yours as well.'

'At your age…'
'At your stage…'
'When Dad was a lad…'
'We had so much less, but we loved what we had.'

'We both feel quite sorry for youngsters today.
 So much has gone that we had in our day.'

# GUILT

Last week, I was promoted
To manage Rentokil.
They're giving me a party,
But now my daughter's ill.

I long to leave work early,
They've warned me not to go -
'You know the client's coming,
That means you have to show.'

The party's at five thirty,
The speech will be at seven,
And if there's dinner after
I'm stuck until eleven.

I'll earn a lot more money,
The deadlines will be hell -
But what about my daughter,
And worse, if she's not well?

I think of her at eighteen,
And what she wants to be.
I'll live in fear she'll disappear -
'Well, you weren't there for me.'

# UNI

Darling Mum, life's pretty cool.
It's much, much better than at school.
But could you send more money, please?
And thanks for the tuition fees.

It costs a fortune, all the clubs,
And all the drinks in all the pubs.
And then, of course, I have to dress.
You'd hate it if I looked a mess.

And though it's great to have your car,
You know what petrol prices are,
And parking's not exactly free,
And neither is the MOT.

That's not to count the rent for digs
And entry tickets for the gigs,
And forking out for bed and board
Each time I want to go abroad.

Oh yes, for all the parties, too -
A mass of them, the whole term through.
You simply can't get in the queue
Without a bottle, maybe two.

I have to say that Lloyds just laughed
When I proposed an overdraft
Of twenty grand or somewhere near
To cover just this student year.

So once again I'm on my knees,
And begging you to help me, please.
And, Mum, don't send the dosh too late -
A credit transfer would be great.

## PARADISE WOULD BE...

A whole day on my own,
No-one on the telephone,
No meals to cook, except for me,
My choice of programmes on TV,
No clothes to pick up from the floor,
No people pouring through the door,
The time to sort a few things out,
The peace of no-one else about,
The chance, perhaps, to take a look
At some new film, or some old book
I've had for years but never read
And spend all afternoon in bed,
To think of no-one else but me,
How heavenly all that would be!

But families come at quite a price.
What mother gets to Paradise?

# IV

# THEY WON'T EVER CHANGE

'She smiled at you, but not me too'

# THE PHILANDERER

She entered the room.
That smile,
Her bloom,
That old familiar sense of doom.

I saw her standing by the door.
That look,
I'd seen it all before.
A look intended just for you,
God only knows, it's nothing new.

She wanted you -
So plain to see,
That look, that smile was not for me.

I did not comment -
Not my style,
Or intimate I'd seen the guile
Behind those eyes and focused smile.
Again, I stood there by your side,
And buried pride,
And buried pride.

She smiled at you,
But not me too.
She didn't care about us two.

I waited, watched for what you'd do,
The way you looked at her,
I knew.

# THE TUNNEL AT THE END OF THE LIGHT

I know a chap whose every breath
Is guaranteed to bore to death.
My nickname (only in my mind)
Is 'Tunnel'. Yes, it's most unkind.

When Tunnel comes, I have to go.
It's often very rude, I know,
But every word and each remark
Immerses me in sudden dark.

The light goes off when he walks in;
The tunnel's long and dark and thin;
I'm trapped and squeezed and can't get out
As long as Tunnel is about.

What makes the man a greater pain
Is knowing that he'll come again -
A colleague of my spouse, you see;
He has to come here frequently.

# WHEN MEN ARE ILL

When men are ill, they take each pill
As if they're on the point of dying.
They seem to have a special skill
Of groaning, moaning, choking, sighing.
'I wonder what it is?' they'll say.
'It's so much worse than yesterday.'
'It's nothing,' say frustrated spouses
Fed up with witnessing their houses
Set out with every sort of pill
To rectify some minor ill.
At which point, men become more terse,
And end up feeling even worse.
The fact that women, tougher stuff,
Take minor ailments on the cuff
Is lost upon their sea of ills
And even greater sea of pills.

# TWO MEN FRIENDS COMPARE NOTES

*John:*

John thinks, because I have no wife,
I lead the most fantastic life.
'You lucky chap', he says to me,
'A bachelor and fancy free!'
He pictures models in my bed
In scanty slips of shocking red,
And dinners in romantic places
And girls with gorgeous legs and faces.

*Dick:*

Dick thinks, because I have a wife,
I lead the most fantastic life.
He thinks my wife is always able
To put my dinner on the table,
And always pours the perfect gin,
And knows what drawers my socks go in,
And keeps our house all spick and span.
He tells me, 'You're a lucky man.'

*John:*

The truth is different. With no wife,
I lead a very simple life.
I'm usually in bed by ten,
I must admit, alone again.
There's not a model on the scene.
I don't think there has ever been.
Except, of course, my model plane.
In truth, my life is very plain.
And as for slips in shocking red,
I've never seen one in my bed.

*Dick:*

The truth is different. With a wife,
I lead a very simple life.
My wife is often not about,
And doesn't leave my dinner out.
She's into yoga and Pilates
And always whizzing off to parties.
I watch TV, I pour my gin,
I know what drawers my socks go in.
Our house is rarely spick and span.
We muddle through, as best we can.

Without a wife, or with a wife,
We dream about each other's life.

## IN A RESTAURANT

They never said a single word,
The couple sitting by our side;
Maybe our never-ending tide
Of words was simply not their way,
And they found all our talk absurd
And wished us twenty feet away.

Perhaps they did communicate,
But in a very different way.
Or maybe they had lots to say
But not that evening, not right then.
Or else perhaps the day had come
When any words were much too late,
And both had turned to deaf and dumb.

# FACEBOOK

I'm Julie Driscole, with an 'e',
I think you may have heard of me.
My husband left a massive stash -
And, better still, in ready cash.

He married me at eighty-five,
And now, of course, he's not alive.
He left me with a sockin' mountain.
It's three years on, and I'm still countin'.

He left me zillions in his will.
His family pursue me still.
No matter that they say I'm trash,
As I'm the one with Daddy's cash.

It doesn't matter what they say,
As I can always pay my way.
However much his sons condemn,
I pay my lawyers more than them.

I'm Julie Driscole, with an 'e'.
Why not consider dating me?
Well, if you're over eighty-three,
Or else, at least, an OAP.

# THE NEGLIGÉE

My husband likes a book in bed -
He'll read til half past three.
And as for what I wear (or not) -
'You look alright to me.'

He hardly ever gives me flowers,
And if he buys a card,
It simply says 'With love from me' -
A message? Far too hard.

He never buys me pretty things
Like lacy negligées -
Last Christmas my poor sister tried
To change his stuffy ways.

She saw one in a local shop
And tried to drag him in.
He stood there frowning, knitted brows,
His hand up to his chin.

'Oh, Liz would love that!' she implored,
'And no, she's not too old.'
And what did my romantic say?
'But wouldn't she be cold?'

I'll never ever change the chap,
I never even try.
I'd hate to live with someone else,
But often wonder why.

# STRANGE PEOPLE

They are foreigners,
And speak a different language.
They talk about what they do,
Not what they feel.
That is their custom.

They are tribal.
They meet together in groups with a common interest,
And more often than we do,
Sometimes in their thousands
To watch things we hate.

They have a different sense of humour.
They tell jokes more than we do,
And laugh at things we don't find funny,
Mostly us.

They are a stubborn breed,
Struggling to understand us,
And it can be hard to reach them.
We are more open, more accessible.

They do strange things, things we wouldn't,
But not the things we want them to do.
And they do not remember things that we do.
That is not their way.

They are an ancient race, proud of their history,
Threatened by change, territorial,
And fearful their world will be taken away.
Many see us as enemies.

They are constantly looking back
While we look forward,
Longing to be left in peace
To do the things they always did without question,
And it can take a lifetime to understand them.

Strange people, men.


## THE WITTER OF OUR DISCONTENT

'Do I remember 9/11?
Of course, I shop there all the time.
It's pricey though, I'm sure you know.
Not like the good old Five & Dime.'

'The wedding? Oh, sheer purgatory.
Quite honestly, I could have died -
Imagine if the hat you chose
Was on the mother of the bride!'

'Last week I saw The Magic Flute.
You know the song about the comb?
It made me want to change my hair
And find a salon nearer home.'

'The last bit? Can't remember it.
I'd had enough before Act Three,
I spent the whole time worried sick
My car would fail its MOT.'

'I don't think opera's quite my scene,
And since you mention 9/11,
Let's pen that in our diaries now -
Our house, for drinks and pix at seven?'

# V

# A WOMAN'S LOT

'What do you do if a girlfriend gets hitched
to a terrible man?'

## WAITING

I am waiting for someone else to cook dinner.
I am waiting for someone else to lay the table.
I am waiting for someone else to wash up.
The problem is, I'm still waiting.

## AMBITION

The times you tell me that I can't
Are when I feel that I most can.
I'd never tell you that you can't,
But then, I wasn't born a man.

The times you tell me that you could,
I may well feel that I could, too,
But since I wasn't born a man,
I'd never dream of telling you.

# A WOMAN'S LOT

An instant way a chap can blot
His copybook, all chances shot,
And turn me off, right on the spot,
Is when he says 'A woman's lot'.

That ugly phrase, 'A woman's lot',
Says life's a burden, when it's not.
What shameless, condescending rot -
We rather like the lot we've got.

Worse still, that phrase, 'A woman's lot'
Suggests a woman's lot is not
As nice as what the chaps have got,
And smacks of misery and grot.

I hate those words, 'A woman's lot',
And if I'm ever on the spot
When some chap says it - end of plot.
My type of guy? I know he's not.

Perhaps I am a silly clot
To bristle so, when out they trot
With that dire phrase, 'A woman's lot',
But deep down, somehow, I think not.

What woman says 'A woman's lot'?
I don't know one,we'd rather not.
Thank God the phrase is now less hot,
Men don't like a resounding 'What?'

Each time it's said, 'A woman lot'
It somehow says we'll go to pot,
And somewhere, one day, lose the plot,
And men who say it should be shot.

## CHECKOUT

There's a girl at the checkout
With such an odd face,
Her nose far too long
And her eyes out of place.

She's gawky, she's thin,
With impossible hair,
And each time I see her
I'm grateful she's there.

There's always a greeting,
Then flash, comes that smile.
And each time I see it,
I think for a while.

I know that I'm lucky -
My life is in place,
And also, thank goodness,
The eyes in my face.

Yet still I have demons
And still get depressed,
While she's always smiling
And giving her best.

I'd love her to know
Her smile has such power.
Much better than seeing
The shrink for an hour.

# CONTENTMENT

My older sister has more style,
My younger one a warmer smile.
My brother has a sharper wit,
And I don't mind, I live with it.

My best friend has a lot more money,
She also tends to be more funny.
Her flat is far more grand than mine.
My place, however, suits me fine.

I do not look at magazines
And wish I looked that good in jeans,
Or ever envy model faces,
And dream of one day changing places.

At work, there's never been a day
I envy other people's pay,
Or times I feel a sense of loss
If someone else is made the boss.

But am I somehow lacking passion
With envy in such meagre ration?
And would my life be better spent
If I were not so damned content?

I have enough; I don't want more,
Commendable? I'm not so sure.
These days it seems a deadly sin
To settle for the life you're in.

# IMPULSE

I knew the car I wanted,
But chose another one.
And why? I loved the colour;
I thought it looked more fun.

I plan a supper party;
I work out what to do,
And then, when I go shopping,
I think of something new.

I go to buy a saucepan.
I end up with a dress.
But is that so unusual?
It is to men, I guess.

I've still not got the saucepan,
And now don't like the dress.
I'll buy the pan tomorrow…
Unless, unless, unless.

# MULTI-TALKING

You say I never listen.
I do, but talk as well,
And do the two together -
A habit you find hell.

I talk and watch the telly,
And still take in the plot.
You have to sit in silence,
Or else you miss the lot.

I flit around ten subjects,
You concentrate on one.
And I go off at tangents,
A thing you've never done.

And when folks come to dinner,
And I join in the din,
You raise your hand for silence
Until they listen in.

You love it when they ponder
On every word you've said,
And if they interrupt you,
You soon slope off to bed.

Of all the ways we're different,
The way we talk is one,
And while it so frustrates you,
I find it rather fun.

## GOD'S DESIGN STUDIO

I'd like to meet God and ask the old bod -
I'm sorry if that sounds ungodly -
Just why he chose men to pick up the pen.
'You must have, they drew us so oddly.'

I'd tell the dear Lord, 'Your thinking was flawed.
It's obvious women weren't present,
Because if they were, I'm sure you'd concur
That congress might well be more pleasant.

Dear God, why employ a man or a boy
To finish a concept so vital?
A woman would know where things should all go,
And Studio Head is your title?

I've always thought God is terribly odd
To dream up some great bits and pieces,
But then, before long, go horribly wrong
Designing the gentler of species.

The clitoris? Yes, I have to confess
That this time your concept was splendid.
But then, yet again, you left it to men,
And there the whole miracle ended.

Out there? It's a joke. What girl wants a bloke
If the fellow can't find its position?
Within the vagina would be so much finer,
Is that beyond male intuition?

And who finished chests, and put on our breasts
In sizes like 44D?
Sorry, no prizes for boobs of such sizes
Or anything much over B.

And what chap surmised that breasts could be prized
As objects of sexual attention,
Yet suckle as well? The concept's from hell,
And hardly a thoughtful invention.

And who drew a spot, if myth it is not,
That no-one discovered for ages?
It's all so unfair that women weren't there
To sign off design at all stages.'

I'd say, 'Your art courses means loads of divorces
And all kinds of angst and frustration.
With women on board, we could be assured
Of instant success and elation.

Without satisfaction, the female reaction
Is looking elsewhere for sensation.'
I hope and I pray that what you won't say
Is, 'Yes, it boosts world population.'

## WOMEN'S GROUPS

There's nothing wrong with women's groups,
Except they're wrong for me.
The concept somehow sits at odds
With my mentality.

I've never joined a women's group
Or any kind of club.
And when I meet my women friends,
We tend to choose the pub.

I love to talk with women friends
In groups of two or three,
But somehow, larger female groups
Feel oddly wrong for me.

I don't mind working in a group -
For charity, maybe,
But shrink from an all-female cast.
Is something wrong with me?

I'm hardly anti-women's things.
It's not as if I'm shy,
Or else confused about my sex,
Or even slightly bi.

But am I so unusual?
I look around and see
A thousand other womenfolk
Who feel the same as me.

Well, have you joined a women's group,
Or any kind of club?
The chances are, you're just like me -
I'll meet you in the pub.

# DOUBLE LIFE

'Er, weekends?  No, impossible -
I'm never ever free.'
The months roll on, he's always gone -
Not one weekend with me.

I ask him why, he gives a sigh,
'It's work, too much to do.
I have to work, and each weekend,
To leave the time for you'.

I call, we talk, I email him;
There's often one he sends,
Which always comes within the week,
But never at weekends.

I love him, I put up with it,
We meet three times a week,
And then one day, an email comes
Which sorts out the mystique.

'I'm sorry, but you ought to know
He's lived for years with me.
He's always had a roving eye,
Some other girl he'll see.

I found your emails yesterday,
And thought I'd better say.
Take my advice, get shot of him,
And send him on his way.

It suits me, having time alone -
So yes, I'm part to blame,
But reading what you've sent to him
I know you're not the same.

Tell him you know, and I know too,
And end it all today.
Well, after all, it's mid-week now,
You've got til Saturday.

And do you have his dressing gown?
The cashmere one? It's lost.
Please tell the brute to bring it back.
Or give me what it cost'.

## A WASTE OF TIME

You meet, but don't have sex for months,
And then what? He's disaster.
And what an awful waste of time,
You wish you'd known much faster.
Of course, the fellow might improve
With time, and so might you.
But usually a female knows
At once if that's not true.
However did our forebears wait
For all those years to wed,
And then discover that their man
Was terrible in bed?
Then hope and pray that years away
One day he'd learn to do it,
But know somehow, it's too late now -
They took a chance, and blew it.

# LOVE HER, LOATHE HER CHAP

What do you do if a girlfriend
Gets hitched with a terrible man?
Glue on a smile and say nothing?
See her alone if you can?

Whatever you do will be hopeless,
Whatever you say, she will guess.
And after a while you won't see her,
As she'll want to see you much less.

No matter how clever an actress,
No matter your lies, she will guess;
Your friendship is doomed, and quite quickly.
I'd give it a year, more or less.

# BITCH

Her nose has been done,
I'm quite sure of that.
Her lips have been filled,
They're bee-stung, too fat.

Her hair is too blonde,
A gallon of bleach.
And as for her tan,
It's not from the beach.

She's just had a lift,
Her skin looks all tight,
And goodness, those teeth!
Impossibly white.

Her dress is too tight,
Her cleavage too low,
And heavens, what boobs -
They're stars of the show.

An obvious job,
Too rounded by far.
Huge semi-circles
Bulge out of her bra.

I guess at her age,
Around fifty-nine.
Her hands are the clues,
Exactly like mine.

She's pleasant, she's charming,
She seems to like me.
I give her a smile -
What a bitch I can be.

## WOLF WHISTLE

The whistle thrilled me, I can say.
I thought 'Not bad, at fifty-three!'
And turned around to see the chap
Whose compliment so flattered me.

And there he was, atop a house,
Some fifty, sixty feet above,
And when he saw my smiling face,
The fellow said, 'Oh sorry, love!'

Of course, I realised straight away
He didn't mean to be unkind
Or spoil my day in any way.
He'd only seen me from behind.

## JUST ONE THING

I've never ever been the boss,
I've never run the show -
Except at supper parties here
For people whom I know.

I've never played the leading part
On any wider stage,
And can't see that I'll ever change -
You don't when you're my age.

I've never tried to write a book,
I'm hopeless with a pen.
I did once join a painting class,
But never went again.

I guess I'm not that bad a cook,
I make a decent dinner.
But make it on to Masterchef?
I'd never be a winner.

I do the crosswords in the Mail,
That's how I start the day,
But gaze with awe at friends of mine
Who do them straight away.

Sudoku? Yes, I do that too,
Though numbers aren't my thing.
I simply wish I did things well -
Bridge, tennis, anything.

I keep the house and garden nice,
I do that pretty well,
But how I long for just one thing
At which I could excel.

# WHAT IN HELL TO DO NEXT?

I used to work, but can't go back.
I could, but I would get the sack.
I'm in my fifties, out of touch -
Well, everything has changed so much.

I work from time to time today -
Theatre group not far away,
But go there each and every day
While no-one is prepared to pay?

Hell no, I'd rather pay my way
And can't float round the house all day.
But what to do? But what to do
With thirty years ahead of you?

My sister runs a B&B -
That's fine for her, but not for me.
Those endless sheets to strip and clean?
I'm sorry, but that's not my scene.

My best friend is a volunteer -
A Wetlands centre, somewhere near.
I couldn't cope with birds all day
Or guiding twitchers on their way.

My cousin's taken up the pen
Just like so many older men.
I often think, round sixty-two
They cannot think what else to do.

While he attempts to write a book
I could become a better cook,
But then, I've never been that keen
On any kind of haute cuisine.

My neighbour's busy touring Asia,
And has a villa in Croatia.
Oh yes, I also like to roam,
But not because I'm bored at home.

And anyway, my husband works,
He's in the office every day,
So if we bought a place abroad
He'd hardly ever get away.

And then there is my great mate Annie,
Who seems to be a full-time Granny
And seems to revel in her role -
But then, she's a maternal soul.

My sister sometimes says to me
'Well, why not help a charity?'
My problem is, despite the cause,
I find committee people bores.

And then, there's Joan, forever cleaning.
I always think that's so demeaning.
Whatever else, one thing I know -
That's not a route that I will go.

Like lots of older, aimless spouses,
Joanna's always moving houses.
As soon as one is barely done
She's off to find another one.

If only I had one great skill
With so much time ahead to kill.
I don't, so what on earth to do?
I only wish I knew. Do you?

# VI

## SENIOR MOMENTS

'Today we potter arm in arm -
It gives us a nice sense of calm'

# I WISH

Love today is far from blind.
In fact, it sees too well,
Which makes us fear the loss of it,
And growing older, hell.

Love spots too many flaws today,
Each tiny imperfection,
Which means, these days, it often strays,
Or dwindles to affection.

What fellow said that love was blind?
I only wish it were.
My plastic surgeon costs a bomb
Because I don't concur.

## LOST FOR WORDS

A mouse to me is still a thing
That scampers round the skirting board,
And surfing makes me think of times
We went on holidays abroad.

To me a blackberry's a plant,
And not a sort of mobile phone,
And apple is another fruit,
I know, because I grow my own.

Orange? That's a nice bright shade,
Or else it's just another fruit.
And booting up is what we did
On rainy days or at a shoot.

Explorer used to be a chap
Like Stanley, Livingstone or Scott.
Whatever else it means today,
Intrepid hero it is not.

To me a menu's still a thing
You saw when you went out to eat,
Although I seldom see them now
As dinner out is quite a treat.

And logging used to be a trade
In woods and forests far away.
But blogging, what on earth is that?
I'm lost in what words mean today.

Sky used to mean an arc of blue,
Perhaps a fluffy cloud or two,
But now it means a TV choice
With far too many things to view.

An iPod? Sounds just like a plant -
A pod, to me, suggests fresh peas.
And as for what a Facebook means,
Could someone out there tell me, please?

A net to me still catches fish,
And web is what a spider's in,
And desktop means exactly that.
These days, we oldies cannot win.

## I GO TO BED WITH SYLVIA PLATH

I love her in bed, dear Sylvia Plath -
She sends me to sleep right away.
I can't understand a word that she says,
I read half a poem a day.

I used to have problems going to sleep,
But now I nod off in a wink.
Dear Sylvia's brilliant,
Much better than pills -
I've chucked the whole lot down the sink.

# COMFORTABLE

Long-term husbands are like cosy old armchairs.
They grunt and creak a bit, but you don't mind.
They're still a comfort when you slump down exhausted.

It's nice to lean against them,
Though they're frayed at the edges.
You can't be bothered to alter them. It's too late,
And anyway, you've got used to the way they are.
You even quite like their time-worn upholstery.

They sit there in front of the fire or the telly
Like familiar islands, waiting for you,
Sometimes afraid that you'll squash them
Back into place,
But mostly glad you're there.

Some of their stuffing may have gone,
But not their charm,
And not their ability to sit silently
And give you a sense of calm when you're troubled.

These days, their legs may be a bit unsure,
But no matter, you're not going to move them too far.
They're happy where they are,
And they're not going to walk.

You can pat them down, plump them up,
Re-arrange them a bit,
And feel relieved that they support you
In a world gone mad.
You love them,
You've lived together so long.

# TWO VERY OLD MEN FRIENDS

'Good morning, Mike!' 'Good morning, Pete!'
'How very nice that we could meet.'
'But my name's John.' 'And mine is Don.'
'Well, never mind, let's carry on.'

'And how's your wife, the lovely Jean?'
'She's fine. Of course, you mean Irene.'
'Of course! And how is Isabelle?'
'Oh, Anne is fine. She's very well.'

'You still play golf? The same old club?'
'Oh no. These days, I'm in the pub.
My local is the Rose and Crown.
It's somewhere in this part of town.'

'I know. It's here. It's where we are.
The name is just above the bar.'
'Oh, so it is! I see it now.
I thought we chose the Spotted Cow.'

'So how are things?' 'Fine, can't complain.
We've just come back from France…no, Spain.
A little villa by the sea.
The place escapes my memory.'

'How nice! We've also been away.
We only got back yesterday.
Oh no…perhaps the day before.
I can't remember any more.'

'It's really nice to see you, Pete.
I'm really glad that we could meet.'
'Well, Mike, I'll say the same to you.
Now, how about a beer or two?'

# THE DANCE OF TIME

Remember how we used to kiss?
I have to say, I do not miss
Those explorations of the jaw.
Today, it's hugs, but little more.

Remember strolling hand in hand,
Exploring some far distant land?
Today, we potter arm in arm -
It gives us a nice sense of calm.

Remember how we used to dance,
And twirl and swirl and preen and prance -
And all night long - til three or four?
Today, it's safer off the floor.

Remember how you stroked my hair,
When thick and long and Nordic fair?
That's over, now my thinning mop
Can only take a shorter crop.

Remember how you used to say
'I love you', each and every day?
Today you do, but once a week,
And add a peck upon my cheek.

Remember how it used to be?
I do, but not regretfully.
We're deep companions - that's the bliss.
I think, at best, it comes to this.

## WHAT AM I DOING HERE?

I'm learning bridge,
I fill the fridge,
I ride, I read the Telegraph,
I garden, cook, I walk the dog,
And look good for my other half.

I go to films,
Find things to do,
I help a charity or two,
I go to London now and then,
And catch the fast train back again.

I do a decent barbecue,
I cope with eight or forty-two,
I often ask the children down -
I think they need a break from town.

My friends come round, I find that fun.
Each month, I get my highlights done.
I rent a cottage, see to that,
Make sure I never get too fat.

I travel four, five times a year,
I've found a kennel nice and near,
I read a bit, though not enough -
It's normally detective stuff.

I hotmail photos, family news,
I go to all the usual dos -
The weddings, christenings, things like that,
Each new excuse to wear a hat.

I'm in good health at sixty-three,
I know that life is kind to me.
I count my blessings when I see
Those ghastly programmes on TV.

And yet I lie awake at night
And know that something isn't right.
I fill my time, I have my friends,
But wish that wasn't where it ends.

# IVF

Hello, I'm Anne, I'm sixty-one,
And this is Josh, my baby son.
My other children, Jane and Lee,
Are thirty-eight and thirty-three.
I know just what you think of me.

I'd like to state most forcibly
That Jane and Lee supported me
When I first went for IVF,
As did my second husband, Geoff.
He'd never had a child, you see.
I thought it only fair of me.

A million times we've thought ahead,
And asked, 'What happens when we're dead?'

I reckon I'll make ninety-one,
And how old would that make my son?
Well, thirty. Not a tender age.
Who needs a mother at that stage?

I feel that I am at my peak.
There's nothing wrong with my physique.
I do not smoke, I do not drink.
And yes, I know just what you think.

You think that I will look a fool
When taking him to nursery school,
And worse, you say that so will he
To have a Mum of sixty-three.

You think he'll always be embarrassed,
Or worse still, bullied, teased and harassed
And find his life a constant test.
Oh yes, and I can guess the rest.

You say that when he's in his teens
I won't be up to all the scenes
And all that adolescent stuff.
You're wrong. I'm strong, and tough enough.

And ask yourself, what if we go
When he is twenty-one or so?
He'll get the house, he'll have the lot,
And much more than you ever got.

You ask him then, from year to year
'Now, would you rather not be here?'

# THE MORNING AFTER

Last night, our best friends came to dinner,
They left at a quarter past two.
But what did we say to each other?
It's dreadful, I haven't a clue.

I'm sure that the evening was lovely.
I'm certain it went with a swing.
But what did we say round the table?
I barely remember a thing.

I seem to recall that we argued,
But what did we argue about?
It can't have been all that important,
Perhaps I should call to find out.

The saucepans are pleasingly empty,
There's nothing much left of the pud.
Did no-one once mention the dinner,
And say that my cooking was good?

Perhaps we've met rather too often,
And said all the same things before.
Perhaps we said nothing that mattered,
Or can't hear as well any more.

It must have been pleasantly jolly -
The bottles give that much away.
But what in God's name did we talk of ?
Whatever did anyone say?

## SIXTIES

The greatest joy today is meeting
Women who are not competing.
Well, women the same age as me -
And I admit to sixty-three.

Of course, a few have found success,
While others made a bloody mess.
There comes a time when no-one cares
Or tries to put on special airs.

We've reached a stage when we can share
Without temptation to compare,
With no restraint and no attrition -
It's gone: suspicion, inhibition.

I had to wait til thirty-four
To like most women more and more.
And as the future years progressed,
I found most women at their best.

Whatever else has gone, I know
I do not yearn for long ago,
Or dream of being young again,
Competing for the decent men.

We do not have our youthful faces,
But ageing deals us other aces.
Friends and sisters, singles, wives -
These days, we don't compare our lives.

## SENIOR MOMENTS

I've gone upstairs,
But why?
What for?
I pause beside the bedroom door.

To find my specs?
No, on my head.
Was it perhaps
To make the bed?

To change a light bulb?
No, they're on,
And not a single one has gone.

To find my book?
No, that's downstairs.
To hang the clothes tossed on the chairs?

I sit awhile upon the bed.
I think, I frown, I scratch my head.

To close a window?
Fetch my pen?
Oh dear, I'd better start again.

## DONE IN

Done glam,
Done that,
Affairs and marriage,
Done children - two,
And one miscarriage.
Done jobs,
Done moving,
Five, six houses.
Done dramas, problems,
Done two spouses.
Done student stuff,
The usual thing,
Done bailing out
And everything.
Done mortgages,
Done place abroad,
Done best I could
And could afford.
Done dinner parties,
Folks to stay,
Done crowds of them
On Christmas Day.
Done Granny things,
Done babysitting,
Done christenings,
Birthdays,
Done the knitting.
Done bridge,
Done coach trips,
Done art courses,
Done family problems -
Two divorces.
Done cooking meals for everyone,
Done microwaving food for one,

Done heating things all soft and runny,
Done meals on wheels, done milk and honey.
Done teeth, done bridges,
Done the lot,
Done what I can for those I've got.
Done aches and pains,
Done two new hips.
Done endless, countless clinic trips.
Done funerals,
Done far too many,
These days, my dearest,
Two a penny.
Done ninety years,
And is it fun?
Done in - can't face another one.

## 'DO SIT DOWN, EVERYONE!'

There was a time, too long ago
Where everywhere that I would go
Men checked to see a space was free -
And on the chair next door to me.
No longer, as the years unfold -
Today I'm old. Today, I'm old.
The younger men now hesitate,
Or look around if asked to wait,
And take a chance if they are able
To sit elsewhere around the table.
They like my wisdom, yes maybe,
But not to sit next door to me
As once they did, way in the past.
Those times have passed,
Those times have passed.
I know I shouldn't mind a bit
They only like my ready wit,
But all the same, it's hard to feel
Your total lack of sex appeal,
And make your humour take the place
Of what was once your lovely face.

# SHOWROOM

'I want something new,
Something bang up to date
And easy to get around in….

Something fun and fast,
And sleek and streamlined,
That people admire whenever I pass them….

Something that sails around corners,
Overtakes effortlessly
And doesn't need constant repairs…..

Something safe and responsive,
Utterly reliable and a joy to be inside….

Something that never lets me down,
Always gets going first thing,
And that I never have to worry about….

Something that does what I ask it to, automatically,
And does it every time without any trouble ….

I want something new, not high maintenance
Like this creaking old heap
With its grunts and groans…

What I want is a brand new body'.

# GOD, YOU'RE ELUSIVE

We never talk any more.
I go to your house
And knock on the door,
But you're not there,
Or you never answer.

We were close once, remember?
When I was married,
When my daughter was born,
When I had my first garden.
You talked to me for hours
While I was tending the flowers.
And then you disappeared out of my life.

Years later, I saw you by the river.
I was watching a kingfisher.
A sudden spear of brilliant blue
Slicing the water.
And swooping upwards
With a silvery fish,
Sparkling and shaking
In the summer sunlight.
The moment was heaven,
And suddenly you were there.
We were walking the same path.

And now you never call.
I don't see you at all.
Even when my partner died
I tried to get in touch,
But you did not come.

Oh yes, I see you at weddings, christenings
And funerals,
But you're always too busy talking
To someone else.

God, you're elusive.
I am losing my faith in you.
Maybe we should go our separate ways.
But perhaps you'll be there for me
In the end.

# NO COMMENT

These days, I keep a store of zips.
They're pretty handy things for lips.